KU-561-358

EXPLORING THE WORLD OF
Wolves

Tracy C. Read

FIREFLY BOOKS

A FIREFLY BOOK

Published by Firefly Books Ltd. 2010

Copyright © 2010 Firefly Books Ltd.
Text copyright © 2010 Tracy C. Read
Images copyright as noted in photo credits

All rights reserved. No part of this publication may be reproduced, stored in a retrieval system, or transmitted in any form or by any means, electronic, mechanical, photocopying, recording or otherwise, without the prior written permission of the Publisher.

First Printing

Publisher Cataloging-in-Publication Data (U.S.)
Read, Tracy C.
    Wolves / Tracy C. Read.
[24] p. : col. photos. ; cm.
Exploring the world of.
Includes index.
Summary: Fascinating facts
 and full-color photos
ISBN-13: 978-1-55407-646-8 (bound)
ISBN-10: 1-55407-646-3 (bound)
ISBN-13: 978-1-55407-655-0 (pbk.)
ISBN-10: 155407-655-2 (pbk.)
1. Wolves - Juvenile literature.
I. Exploring the world of. II. Title.
599.773 dc22   QL737.C22R43 2010

Library and Archives Canada
  Cataloguing in Publication
Read, Tracy C.
    Exploring the world of wolves /
  Tracy C. Read.
Includes index.
ISBN-13: 978-1-55407-646-8 (bound)
ISBN-10: 1-55407-646-3 (bound)
ISBN-13: 978-1-55407-655-0 (pbk.)
ISBN-10: 1-55407-655-2 (pbk.)
1. Wolves--Juvenile literature. I. Title
QL737.C22R425 2010
j599.773   C2010-900723-9

Published in the United States by
Firefly Books (U.S.) Inc.
P.O. Box 1338, Ellicott Station
Buffalo, New York 14205

Published in Canada by
Firefly Books Ltd.
66 Leek Crescent
Richmond Hill, Ontario L4B 1H1

The Publisher gratefully acknowledges the financial support for our publishing program by the Government of Canada through the Canada Book Fund as administered by the Department of Canadian Heritage.

Cover and interior design by
Janice McLean, Bookmakers Press Inc.
jmclean14@cogeco.ca

Manufactured by Printplus Limited in Shen Zhen, Guang Dong, P.R.China in April, 2010, Job #S100400151

Front cover: © J. Klingebiel/Shutterstock
Back cover: © Stephane Angue/Shutterstock
Back cover, inset, left:
    © Daniel Korzeniewski/Shutterstock
Back cover, inset, right top:
    © Lori Labrecque/Shutterstock
Back cover, inset, right bottom:
    © Chris Alcock/ Shutterstock

CONTENTS

DOWNTIME
A gray wolf takes time out for a cooling roll in the snow after a hard day's hunt.

MEET THE GRAY WOLF

The largest wild member of the dog family, the gray wolf (*Canis lupus*) once roamed much of North America, hunting large hoofed mammals such as deer, caribou, moose and bison. As humans settled in its traditional territories, however, we unleashed a harsh campaign to eliminate the wolf, which we resented for its attacks on big game and, later, on domestic livestock.

By the mid-20th century, efforts to hunt and poison wolf populations had taken a brutal toll in southern Canada and the lower 48 states. Its relative, the red wolf (*Canis rufus*), which once made its home in the southeastern United States, disappeared from the wild. Thanks to conservationists,

gray wolf recovery efforts have now returned healthy breeding populations to some regions, though the wolf still faces an uncertain future. The dedicated work of field biologists has likewise played a vital role in helping us to understand the wolf's place in wilderness ecology.

Its reputation as a fierce predator precedes it, but the wolf is also a social animal, living in groups called packs, in which members share the tasks of hunting and raising the young. Researchers report that these distant ancestors of the domestic dog display many of its traits: playfulness, personality, friendliness and loyalty. From the gray wolf, we'll learn that the drive to succeed can live alongside the animal yearning to connect.

ANATOMY LESSON

From its elongated snout and sharp teeth to the tip of its expressive tail, the gray wolf is designed for hunting and eating meat. This wild dog and its pack spend much of the year on the move in an endless search for large prey such as deer and moose.

All canids are meant to run, but with its narrow chest and powerful back, the wolf is built for distance and endurance rather than speed. It trots across its territory at a steady pace of up to five miles per hour (8 km/h). But when it needs to, it can sprint at speeds approaching 40 miles per hour (64 km/h) and cover 16 feet (4.9 m) in a single bound.

The wolf's long legs give it an edge when moving through the snow that covers much of its range in winter. Big, pliable paws and blunt claws are also an advantage in gripping uneven and icy surfaces.

A thick fur coat with a surface layer of water-repellent guard hairs and a dense moisture-resistant insulating undercoat helps the wolf endure frigid temperatures. The farther north the wolf lives, the heavier its coat. As well, northern wolves are usually bigger than their more southerly cousins.

The wolf's next successful hunt can't be predicted, so once its prey is down, it can't let anything go to waste. Nor does it want to risk losing its dinner to other predators. A large stomach allows it to gorge on some 20 pounds (9 kg) of meat at one time.

BORN TO HUNT

The powerfully built gray wolf is suited for a life on the move, while its sharp, pointed front teeth and massive molars make it an eating machine. Below: The red wolf has short, reddish fur and is smaller than the gray wolf but bigger than the coyote. By the late 1980s, habitat loss and a campaign to eliminate the red wolf from its home in the American Southeast had done their work. Today, this endangered wolf is being restored to its ecosystem through recovery programs.

Physical strength and stamina are key to a wolf's hunting success. To target and track its much bigger prey, a wolf pack roams tirelessly over a large territory.

Eyes
At birth, a wolf cub's eyes are usually blue. By adulthood, they are yellow, gold, green or brownish.

Tongue
Its long, flexible tongue allows the wolf to scoop up big gulps of water.

Teeth
The wolf's 42 teeth include eight bone-crushing molars and four long, sharp fangs, also known as canines.

Big foot
Large paws and long hind legs give the wolf a locomotion advantage over other canids.

Height
On average, a wolf measures from 24 to 37 inches (61-94 cm) at the shoulder.

Grandma, what big ears you have
The wolf is always on the alert for the sound of prey and the low, haunting howl of its packmates.

Stomach
The wolf's large simple stomach can process a huge volume of protein and fat in just a few hours.

Weight
The male weighs from 45 to 175 pounds (20-80 kg); the female, from 40 to 120 pounds (18-55 kg).

Tail talk
Measuring from 13½ to 23½ inches (34-60 cm) long, the tail signals attitude and status. A raised tail means dominance; a lowered tail whimpers "uncle."

VARIETY SHOW

Wolf fur can range in color from gray to gray-brown, buff, brown, white and black — or a combination of all these colors. The ears and nose of the white wolf, which lives in the High Arctic, are slightly shorter to protect them from the cold and wind.

Average lifespan in the wild
6 to 8 years

9

NATURAL TALENTS

Like all wild animals, the gray wolf relies on its five senses — sight, hearing, smell, taste and touch — to navigate its world successfully. Much of that success is based on the wolf pack's ability to find food.

With keen eyesight that seems to be especially responsive to movement, the ever watchful wolf keeps track of its prey as well as its pack. Well-developed hearing alerts the wolf to danger and also allows members of the pack to stay in touch through their trademark howls, which can be heard over great distances.

The wolf's long muzzle plays an important role in the search for food. Not only does the muzzle house the wolf's imposing upper and lower jaws and teeth, which serve as vital hunting and food-processing tools, but it also provides a large space for the wolf's olfactory system. In fact, according to biologists, the physical area devoted to smelling in some members of the dog family is roughly 14 times larger than it is in humans. In turn, the canid's ability to detect odors is almost 100 times more developed than that of a human.

Wolf expert David Mech has reported that a wolf standing downwind can typically smell potential prey some 300 yards (275 m) away. Even more impressive, Mech once witnessed a wolf pack pick up the scent of a moose and her two calves from a distance

ALL EARS, EYES & NOSE

The wolf uses its hearing, vision and sense of smell to hunt and communicate with other wolves.

GOOD LISTENERS

Howling wolves can be heard by other wolves across an area as large as 50 square miles (130 sq km).

of 1½ miles (2.4 km). Once a scent is detected, he writes, the wolves halt, then quickly gather with their noses pressed together, excitedly wagging their tails, before heading off to do battle for their next meal.

The wolf's sense of smell also plays a part in the way individuals within the pack interact. Greet-ings to returning members often feature extensive mutual sniffing. And, like domestic dogs, wolves use scent to mark their territories. By urinating on rocks, pieces of wood and chunks of ice that serve as "scent posts," individuals leave evidence of their presence for their packmates and other wolves.

The wolf's ravenous eating style suggests that the taste of its food does not play a central part in its meal plan. Touch, however, is another matter. In contrast to its savage hunting habits, the wolf regularly explores and indulges its sense of touch with members of its pack through affectionate wrestling, jostling, nuzzling, playing and licking.

SIGHT
The wolf's well-developed vision is especially sensitive to movement.

HEARING
A wolf can hear another wolf howling from at least four miles (6.4 km) away.

SMELL
A wolf's sense of smell is estimated to be 100 times keener than a human's.

TASTE
What tastes like dinner to a wolf? Meat.

TOUCH
A big part of a wolf's social life is its physical interaction with pack members.

PACK MENTALITY

Unlike the solitary fox, the wolf is a social animal that enjoys the benefits of cooperative group living in the wild.

But every team needs a captain. In wolf society, that job is shared by a powerful male wolf (the "alpha male") with enough drive and personality to inspire obedience and loyalty and the strongest, healthiest female (the "alpha female"). Together, this pair brings stability and order to the pack on a daily basis.

A typical wolf pack is a family unit with six to eight members. Besides the alpha couple, members can include unrelated adults of various ages and juvenile and adult offspring of pack members.

The pack itself can change from year to year — members die or are killed or leave to start their own pack. Eventually, the alpha couple is replaced by younger, stronger wolves.

As it is with humans, courtship and mating for the wolf can be complicated. The alpha couple are often, but not always, the parents of the new litter of pups. Before mating, the male and female display affectionate courtship behaviors, including head rubbing, nose bumping and sniffing. The act of mating itself seems to create a deep emotional bond between the pair.

A few weeks before giving birth, the pregnant female, with the help of the pack, digs one or more dens, often situated on high

FAMILY TIES

Whether there are three members or 30, the wolf pack that hunts, plays and howls together stays together.

ground and close to water. Caves, abandoned burrows or hollowed-out trees may also be used. If the pack feels safe, it may return to the same den year after year.

Roughly two months after the early-spring breeding season, the female gives birth to a litter of four to six helpless one-pound (454 g) pups. The mother enjoys home-delivery meals from her pack as she nurses. At three weeks, the pups are playing together outside the den entrance.

Over the summer, the pups are moved to a series of "rendezvous sites," where they are cared for by one or more adults as the others go off to hunt. Through play fighting and wrestling, the pups begin to develop the skills they will later use on the hunt. At the same time, the growing pups forge a loyal connection with the pack.

By autumn, the pack is on the move again, and the education of the juveniles continues. In two years, some are ready to set out on their own; others will stick with the family they know and trust.

PUP PROFILE
At two weeks, the pup's eyes open. By two months, its feet and head look a little too big for its body.

WHO'S THE BOSS?
During their first summer, littermates fight it out to determine who's who in the pack's pecking order.

BEST FRIENDS FOREVER

While some wolf siblings may have less than ideal relationships, others form ties that last a lifetime.

INSTANT MESSAGING

In any group, some individuals will fight for a little more power and status, and wolves are no different. To maintain or restore harmony in the pack, wolves rely on a complex system of communication, reacting to one another through physical postures, facial expressions and vocalizations.

The alpha male may impose discipline in the form of physical aggression. Sometimes, though, it takes as little as a "fixed stare" and a raised tail to shut down a weaker wolf. An upright tail, a furrowed brow, a display of sharp teeth and a deep growl can push the threat up a notch.

To signal a willingness to submit to authority, a wolf puts its tail between its legs, lowers its head, pulls its ears back, licks the superior wolf's muzzle or rolls onto its back. An alpha male is greeted by his pack with an enthusiastic but respectful group nuzzle.

The wolf's vocal repertoire includes a whimpering whine, a warning growl and a bark that signals an alarm or a threat. The most famous wolf sound, of course, is its howl, which is used to keep in touch with the pack, to claim territory and to express eagerness before a hunt. One biologist describes it as "a community sing," in which the first howling wolf is joined by excited pack members that throw their heads back and howl for the sheer joy of it. Those who have heard this haunting call say it is unforgettable.

BODY LANGUAGE

Upright tail, bared teeth, a wrinkled forehead and erect ears signal one thing: the dominant wolf is not happy. The smart reply from the weaker wolf? Put your head and tail down, keep your mouth shut and show some respect.

THE HUNT FOR SURVIVAL

As we've learned, humans have played a major role in wiping out gray wolf populations in much of North America. (The same poisoning, hunting and habitat-destruction policies have reduced wolf numbers in Europe and Asia as well.) Today, the majority of North American wolves live in Alaska and northern Canada, also home to the large hoofed mammals that are its prey.

How does the midsized wolf take down animals that are larger, faster and just as quick-witted? In forests, on plains and across the Arctic tundra, the wolf has adapted its way of life to the animals it pursues. Key to its survival is living and hunting in a group, with a strong leader to initiate and oversee the pack's activities. And because wolves hunt plant-eating animals that are in a constant search for something to nibble on, pack members are likewise always on the move.

As the pack patrols its large territory, each member is on the alert for the scent of prey, the chance sighting of an individual or the presence of fresh hoof tracks in the soil or snow. Once a prey animal is detected, the pack switches gears. Its goal now is to get as close as it can without attracting attention. With tails wagging and eyes narrowed, the pack picks up its pace.

How the pack proceeds once the prey sees it depends largely on the prey itself. For instance, a

ENERGY SAVER

A wolf pack patrols vast territories in the North, ranging from 300 to 1,000 square miles (777-2,590 sq km). By trotting over frozen, windswept lakes and rivers, rather than pushing through deep snow, wolves conserve their energy for the hunt.

THIRST QUENCHER

When dinner is a straight-up meal consisting of many pounds of meat, it's important to follow up with a big drink of water to process all that protein and fat. The wolf scoops up H_2O with its long tongue. The pack often picks its den site with a water source nearby.

healthy female moose nudging 800 pounds (363 kg) has good reason to feel confident about challenging a wolf pack. Hard, pointed hooves are powerful weapons, and wisely, the wolf fears them. If the moose walks toward the pack, the wolves may scatter. If the moose stands its ground, the wolves — which don't like eye contact — might linger for a bit and then disperse. But if the moose turns and runs, that's an invitation the pack can't resist. Motion sets off the "rush," with the pack in hot pursuit of its prey. Still, if the pack can't close the gap, it may give up the chase in less than a mile (1.6 km).

Even if the pack makes contact with its prey, a meal isn't a sure thing. Healthy adult mammals with hooves can put up a mighty fight, breaking wolf bones and crushing wolf heads. For this reason, biologists believe the pack has its greatest success when it finds individuals that are weak and sick, old and slow or young and inexperienced and separates them from the herd. They argue that by killing the weakest members of a species, the wolf pack helps keep herds healthy.

In the summer, the pack tends to head out in the evening to hunt, returning by morning. But in winter, the pack is active around the clock, traveling single file through its territory in a never-ending search for food, stopping regularly to rest before moving on again.

WHAT'S ON THE MENU?

Mostly meat. In the Great Lakes region, wolf packs stalk the white-tailed deer; the larger, stronger moose is a second choice. On the Arctic tundra, the caribou, which travels in herds, is on the wolf's radar, while in parts of western and northern Canada, it's elk and Dall's sheep. Solo wolf hunters also have success with beavers, rabbits and rodents.

LONE WOLF

Not every wolf is a member of a pack, as this individual is. Older animals may be driven out, while some young wolves leave and live on their own before finding a partner and starting up a new pack.

PHOTOS © SHUTTERSTOCK

p. 1 Vasily Smirnov

p. 5 Chris Alcock

p. 7 Kirby Morgan

p. 8 Maxim Kulko

p. 9 top: Geoffrey Kuchera

p. 9 middle: fotografie4you

p. 9 bottom: Lori Labrecque

p. 11 Ewan Chesser

p. 13 Geoffrey Kuchera

p. 14 top: Denis Pepin

p. 14 middle: Dennis Donohue

p. 14 bottom: marikond

p. 15 Jeff Grabert

p. 16 top: Eric Isselée

p. 16 middle right: Lori Labrecque

p. 16 middle left: Lori Labrecque

p. 16 bottom: Wolf Mountain Images

p. 17 Cynthia Kidwell

p. 18 top: David W. Kelley

p. 18 bottom: Chris Alcock

p. 19 Ewan Chesser

p. 20 top: Les Palenik

p. 20 middle: Daniel Korzeniewski

p. 20 bottom: Ferderic B

p. 22 top: Daniel Korzeniewski

p. 22 bottom middle: Mike Rogal

p. 22 bottom right: Steve Bower

p. 23 top: Nialat

p. 23 moose: GoodMood Photo

p. 23 elk: Bruce Raynor

p. 23 Dall's sheep: Chris Alcock

p. 23 hare: Nialat

PHOTOS © ISTOCKPHOTO

p. 12 Len Tillim

p. 21 David Parsons

p. 22 bottom left: Neal McClimon

p. 23 beaver: Martina Berg

PHOTOS © WAYNE LYNCH

p. 6